PRAISE FOR

DYING *to* LIVE

How Near Death Experiences Transform Our Faith

"What happens when someone who has given his life prayerfully to help others heal finds he desperately needs healing himself? In this touching, poignant book, Nigel shows the power of prayer in a medical crisis. His story will be sure to help you or anyone you know who needs healing."

—*Rick Hamlin, executive editor,* Guideposts.

"Fr. Nigel Mumford, who has been a personal friend for many years, is a priest with a deep faith in a loving God, who lives out his convictions in real and tangible ways. He has written a very moving account of a profound near-death experience, which is certain to draw the reader not only into his journey, but also into the remarkable visions of heaven he had during that time.

In his own words: "There are times in our lives when we are broken, and there are times or seasons in our lives when we rebuild."

Nigel's simple and down-to-earth way of communicating allows a beautiful transparency of his delightful humor and convincing humanity.

Anyone reading this book will be greatly touched by the loving presence of God, who never leaves us or forsakes us, even in the darkest moments of our lives."

—*Judith and Dr. Francis MacNutt*

"The time Father Nigel was struck ill was a very humbling and fearful time. His illness progressed and he declined so rapidly, it was overwhelming. It made me realize that loved ones can be taken away so quickly and we need to let them know how we feel about them, or we will regret it. I felt God had my role as protector of the Mumford's privacy and support for Lynn. I heard that some folks had called me "pit bull"—and not in an endearing tone. They were frustrated, as everyone wanted information and updates personally.

This time with the Mumfords has cemented our friendship and bond like no other, and the Lord brought us all through it with a renewed faith and trust in Him."

—*Sandra Lester*

"In a world awash with near and post-death stories, Nigel Mumford offers a unique narrative: Unique because it coheres with the biblical witness about our future. Although faith "is the conviction of things not seen," Nigel has taken a peek behind the curtain, and all who read this book will receive the blessing of encouragement in their faith!"

—*Fr. Andrew Buchanan,*
Rector of Galilee Episcopal Church

"It was a 'dark and stormy night' when I received a call stating that this would probably be Nigel Mumford's last night on the earth. My wife and I drove to the hospital, wondering if he would still be alive when we arrived. He was. I administered Last Rites, and we waited. I remember saying, "He's either going to die tonight and go to heaven, or God is going to do a mighty healing that will be a blessing to thousands."

This book, dear friends, is the blessing God has meant - for you and for me!"

—*Bishop David Bena*

Dying to Live:
How Near Death Experiences
Transform Our Faith

by Nigel W. D. Mumford

ISBN 978-1-63393-354-5

Some photos by Diana Haskell photography

Published by

◀ köehlerbooks ™

210 60th Street
Virginia Beach, VA 23451
800-435-4811
www.koehlerbooks.com

DYING
to LIVE

**How Near Death Experiences
Transform Our Faith**

NIGEL W. D.
MUMFORD

VIRGINIA BEACH
CAPE CHARLES

DEDICATION

To my dear bride, Lynn, who had the faith to believe that God would heal me and stayed with me "in sickness and in health" through the very dark valley of the shadow of death for fifty-eight straight days, twelve hours a day, sitting by my bed waiting for the Lord to resurrect and heal me.

And to my dear Family in the UK: my brother Alec, who flew in from England twice to support Lynn when I was in a coma (he tells me he prodded my feet to try and wake me up!); my mum and dad; and my dear sisters, Julie Sheldon and Ann Topping, who were in deep prayer for my very life but unable to travel.

TABLE OF CONTENTS

FOREWORD

We will always be curious of stories about a near–death experience. It's the one thing in life we can't really explain or put clearly into words, yet Nigel manages to convey the magnitude of the visions he experienced while in a coma. Where human words can be inadequate, he beautifully describes how the visions were different than dreams— "More color, more detail, more vibrant, more of everything in life . . . even in death." Nigel paints a picture of heaven that brings comfort, insight, and light, enveloped in a way we can understand and all completely in line with the Word of God. Each vision is so different, so powerful, and so descriptive. I read most of them with tears in my eyes and my mind trying to take in the enormity of what was being imparted to us. These visions need to be taken seriously, to be read and studied, to be talked about, to encourage those crawling through the valley of the shadow that they may run swiftly to the hope that awaits them.

Reading the visions, it becomes apparent that words of life are speaking right through into our hearts; there are gems and jewels to be found, there are treasures waiting in words of revelation, hope, perseverance, expectation, preparation, reality, and the battleground.

I know you will be greatly blessed as you read this book. Nigel has been given an understanding of perseverance in a way we could never imagine, as is expressed so beautifully in Vision 3: "Jesus was pushing me on with his eyes—He wanted me to see the gates."

I pray you will lean into Jesus as you read and allow Him to speak through these visions to bring you encouragement and hope as you persevere in your one and only life on earth.

Dying to Live has been all the more powerful to me because Nigel Mumford is my brother.

JULIE SHELDON
Author, International Speaker & Evangelist,
Pioneer Minister—March 2016

FOREWORD

Everybody has a much loved, larger-than-life friend, and Nigel is one of mine. I'm grateful to God, not just that Nigel survived his traumatic, long-lasting illness that brought him close to death, but that he has been able to put together his reflections on what he experienced.

This account is more than simply a description of his remarkable healing. I found three welcome reminders in it. First, there is the reminder that, to use that image of American baseball, life can pitch us a curveball, and we need to be prepared for it. Most of us who are Christians in the developed world have comfortable lives, cocooned by wealth, technology, and medical science. For most of the time we sail through life on fair-weather seas. The danger here is that we keep God at a distance, and our faith becomes thin and superficial. Yet calm seas and blue skies cannot persist forever. Sooner or later in every life, suffering or loss strikes—sometimes without warning— and when it does, a faith that has been allowed to fade may be found inadequate. Reading this account—and no doubt prompted by Nigel's nautical past—I was reminded of that challenging line of the old hymn, "Will your anchor hold in the storms of life?" Nigel's did. Would ours?

Second, there is a reminder that the Christian God can bring blessing out of suffering. Nigel did not simply survive months of illness, suffering, and bewildering experiences in the grey borderland between life and death; he let God teach him through them. He graduated from the university of adversity. Would we?

Finally, there is an extraordinary reminder of the power of God and how we can access that through faithful prayer. We Christians in the developed world are pressed on every side by secular forces demanding that we conform. Under this unceasing strain, a secular worldview may reduce our belief in God's ability to the point where He is ineffective. In theory, we affirm the supernatural power of God and His ability to do extraordinary things through His Holy Spirit. In practice, when it comes to the crunch, we find that we have little faith that He can answer us in power. Functionally, we have become atheists. This book tells of a man, his family, and friends, who, faced with the severest illness, held on with faith to the expectation that, against the odds, God could heal. This account is a timely, needed reminder that, as James 5:16 tells us, "The prayer of a righteous person is powerful and effective." Nigel and his friends prayed fervently; would we?

Nigel my friend, it's good to have you back with us in the land of the living. And thank you for the lessons for us that you have brought with you.

THE REV. CANON J. JOHN–MARCH, 2016

EARLY LIFE

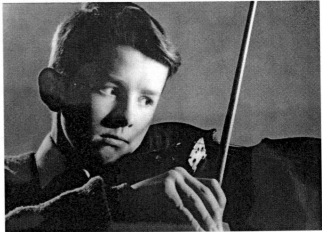

Near Death

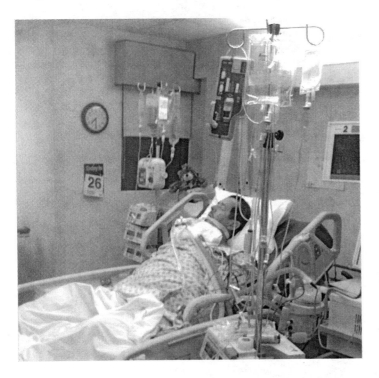

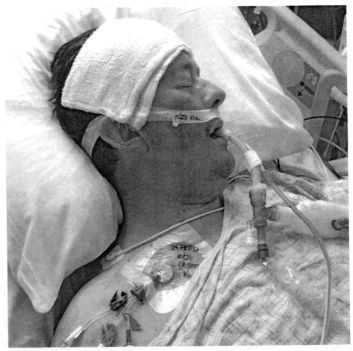

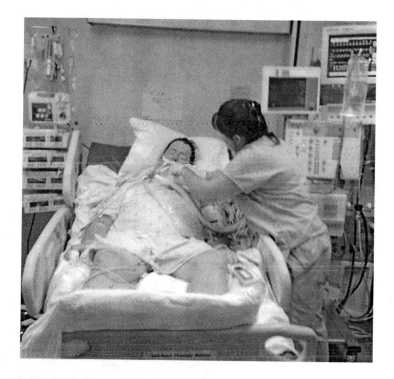

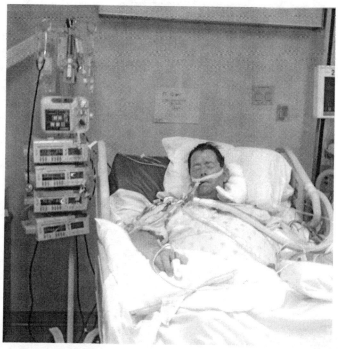

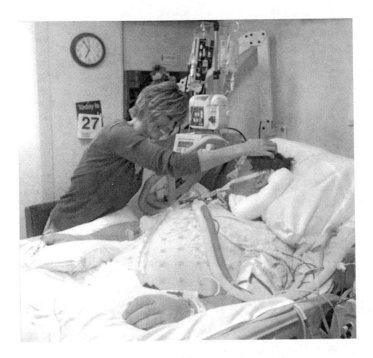

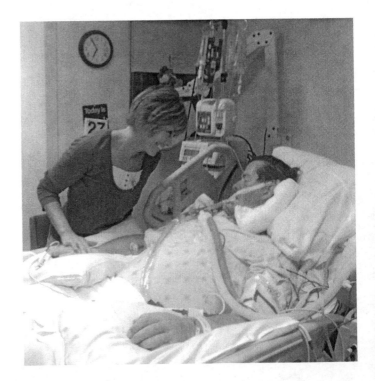

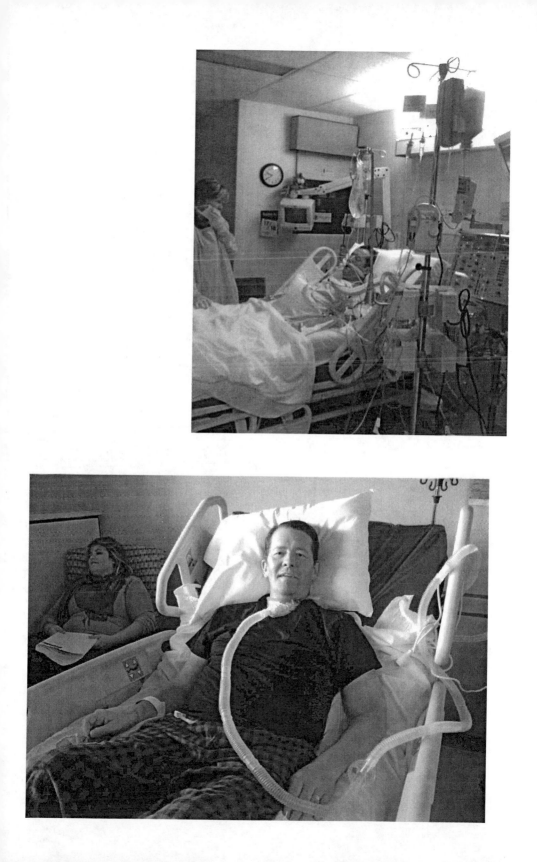

LIFE AFTER

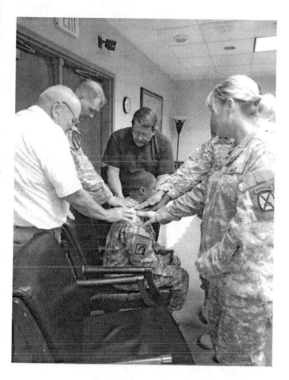

"Hardships often prepare ordinary people for extraordinary destiny."

C.S. Lewis, *A Grief Observed*

PREFACE

I'M ALIVE.

All I can move is my right index finger—nothing else.

Heads move in and out of sight, a kaleidoscope of light around them.

People are speaking. Jaws move, I hear sounds, but I don't understand them.

What has happened to me?

Such were my impressions when I woke from a three—week coma during which I had nearly died. Amazingly, this was not my first near-death experience (NDE.) The other, a drowning, was thirty-seven years earlier.

I've learned so much since then, both through my own close calls with death and through watching others dying in combat, in hospitals, in hospice, and in private homes. I've spoken with people who say they have stepped through the veil of death and then come back.

Each person had a serene, peaceful quality, and each had been through terrible depression trying to come to grips with what had happened. I too am left with a sense of loss, as well as a great peace.

One woman I prayed with for healing of cancer was furious at me. She had sold her car, her house, and all her possessions; and she was ready to go to heaven. Instead, she was totally healed of cancer through prayer. I thought she should have been ecstatic. Instead, she was quite hostile.

"I have nothing," she said.

I thought to myself, "You have everything."

Glimpses of heaven have left me with an understanding, a knowing that in the end it will be well with my soul. That end is actually a beginning, a new experience, an ultimate peace. To be honest, I've put this project aside over and over again. Am I ready to be transparent, open to ridicule and skepticism? Am I ready for those who challenge my experience? Will what I went through help others understand that we don't actually have to fear death when it is our time?

To know life, to stare death in the face—twice—and to come back to write about it— it's a privilege.

Perhaps we all fear death in some fashion, until life events teach us not to fear it at all. Now that I've glimpsed heaven, that fear is gone. I'm left with a sense of peace, a calm knowing that in the end, "All shall be well, and all shall be well, and all manner of things shall be well." (Dame Julian of Norwich, an English mystic, had this vision in 1373.)

I wonder what St. Paul meant when he wrote the verse, "I know a man in Christ who fourteen years ago was caught up to the third heaven. Whether it was in the body or out of the body, I do not know—God knows." (2 Cor. 12:2 NIV)

Was he was writing about himself? Did he have what is now called an "out of body experience?" Did St. Paul have an NDE, a glimpse of heaven? I find this passage so encouraging. It speaks to me, a message from the Grandfather of the Church. I sense peace in his very words.

I hope and pray that this book will help you process the ultimate healing of loved ones. And when it is your time, peace will be understood.

We shall have a perfect night and a peaceful end.

CHAPTER ONE

A Seed of Faith

"Then the Lord God formed a man from the dust of
the ground and breathed into his nostrils the breath
of life, and the man became a living being."
(Gen. 2:7 NIV)

GOD HAS TOUCHED my life in ways I wouldn't
have dreamed possible twenty-five or even ten years ago.
My journey has transformed me from a Royal Marine
Commando and Drill Instructor to a lay healer, then to an
Episcopal priest. I was trained to kill or be killed. Now it is
my calling to train people to heal and be healed.

I was born and raised in Plymouth, UK, where my father
became an Anglican priest. We went to church, of course,
but, as a child, I found it boring. At seventeen, I joined Her
Majesty's Royal Marine Commandos, completed Green
Beret training, and was assigned my first tour of duty in

Belfast, Northern Ireland. In 1972, Belfast was a war-ravaged city. It was just two weeks after Bloody Sunday, a tragic confrontation between the Irish nationalists and the British Army in which many civilians were killed in full view of the public and the press. This was the highest number of people killed in a single shooting incident during the entire conflict.

I was in terrible turmoil. Officially, we were a peacekeeping force. The reality, I knew, would not be peacekeeping, but combat. Two days before going to Ireland, aware I would face mortal danger, I went home for weekend leave. On the way, I met Jesus.

3 P.M., MARCH 10, 1972

It seemed so simple: leaving the train station, stepping into a YMCA, simply getting out of the rain, I was welcomed by a teenager who invited me to the chapel to close my eyes in prayer. When I opened them, the altar was bathed in light, and I felt washed in peace. This moment changed my life, gave me a faith I didn't have. It was a foxhole conversion— without a foxhole. In the short run, I was able to go back to camp ready for anything. In the long run, that seed of faith took root and grew silently inside me, eventually guiding my life.

But in the middle run, I forgot that sense of peace and faith after a few weeks of living in a combat zone. Through three tours in Northern Ireland, a full year of my life, I was hunted by snipers, shot at, blown off my feet by bombings, and blinded by my own blood. I watched my best friend get shot in the street while children kicked in his blood. It is no surprise that I came away a changed man with Post–Traumatic Stress Disorder (PTSD.)

Malta, 1975

In 1975, that seed of faith showed itself again. It was a Sunday morning. Twenty-two years old, I was now on the provost (police) staff of 41 Commando Royal Marines, stationed in Malta. The night before, I'd been out with fellow Royals and had consumed too much "liquid." To be honest, I didn't feel so great, but we had rented a car and planned to rent scuba diving equipment and dive at the Blue Grotto, a beautiful spot.

Our group, eight hungover Marines, went to the dive shop to get kitted out. The Mediterranean was so warm that we didn't need wetsuits, just flippers, tanks, masks, and weight belts. My weight belt felt heavy. We didn't need to sign anything or prove we had dive training. There was a very short briefing, "How to Scuba Dive in Three Minutes." There was one experienced diver among us, but the rest of us had no idea what we were doing.

It was quite an adventure. The beautiful scenery and clear blue water soothed my aching brain. I was thrilled to take my first dive. Adrenalin took over. We were keen to get under the sea! Now looking back, I see this was all an accident waiting to happen. What did I know about scuba? Absolutely nothing. I was about to learn a lot the hard way.

We tried our rented equipment with a couple of test dives in the rocky shallows. The glass of the mask was hazy and scratched, my weight belt was heavy, and the air coming through the mouthpiece smelled old and rubbery.

Then with a pack-like mentality, we all followed the sea's natural slope to the depths. I felt like a budding Jacque Cousteau. It was a fascinating new world.

I was trying to breathe slowly to conserve air as I glided down the underwater valley. It felt like flying in slow motion. Deeper and deeper we went, in total silence, except for sound of the breathing equipment.

One part of the briefing was that we were to be buddied up with another diver. I swam deeper and deeper. At seventy-five feet, I sat cross legged on the sandy bottom. At this point, my dive buddy was out of sight. I was alone in a new world, looking around in wide-eyed amazement. It was far more than I expected.

I wondered how far down I was and what the surface of the water would look like from beneath. So sitting on the sand, I looked up: it resembled a mirrored ceiling. Water leached into my mask and went up my nose. I choked. Since I hadn't been taught how to clear my mask, I had no idea what I to do. I paused, holding my breath, looking toward the mirrored ceiling.

"How do I get from here to the ceiling?" I wondered. I'd seen enough movies of people diving, but had no idea how to "fly" up toward the ceiling. Becoming disoriented, I thought I was sitting cross legged in an ordinary room with a glass ceiling. Could I rise up in the air, break through that glass, and breathe on the other side of the ceiling?

I knew my life was in immediate danger. Pure panic set in. My reaction, I have been told many times, was exactly wrong. I pushed off the sandy bottom with as much force as I could and shot to the surface as fast as possible, with an attitude of "get me out of here!" I kicked my flippers as fast as I could. I seemed to be going up, but it was such work. I reached for the weight belt and tried to remove it. The "quick release" buckle would not open.

As I ascended from the depths, I somehow knew to let air out of my lungs. It just kept coming. I knew I should not breathe in. More and more air kept coming out of my lungs.

Finally, I broke the surface and ripped off the mask, still trying to remove the weight belt. I began to sink. The sea was trying to take me. With as much effort as I could muster, I pushed to the surface and shouted for help. Again I was pulled under by the weight belt. Again I was sinking. Using the drowning man's swim, I managed to get to shore. I tried to crawl out on the jagged rocks as the waves tried to pull me back. The rocky shore was too vertical. As I was dragged back, rocks ripped open the ends of my fingers and shredded my knees. A carpet of sea urchin barbs spiked through my feet. The sea was winning. I just could not get out. I shouted one final plea and let go.

Sinking, I knew I was about to drown. Earlier, as I had opened my mouth to breathe, my mouthpiece, on a single hose, had flipped backwards. Now I'd held my breath for as long as I could, and I put my hand behind my head in one final attempt to grab the air hose. It was nowhere to be found. The sea had won.

This was it, my death, my demise. It was time to involuntarily take a breath of sea water. I waited as long as I could and then breathed in a huge gulp of water, filling my lungs to capacity.

The panic stopped right away. I felt instant peace, the peace that had washed over me in that YMCA chapel. The peace that passes all understanding. Nothing mattered. It was finished.

An old-fashioned slide show began to run, snapshots of my life in chronological order. I remembered that I had known about this phenomenon and that this indeed was supposed to happen. From right to left, the photos streamed faster, faster. My life, in fact, flashed in front of me. It was time to meet my Maker.

Then a vivid yellow light came about me. It formed a yellow tunnel just wide enough for my shoulders. I had the presence of mind to wonder why the yellow tunnel did not go up vertically. Instead, it went horizontally, parallel to the surface of the sea, over the horizon, right toward heaven. I found myself surrounded by the vivid deep yellow of the tunnel. As surely as the sea swallowed me, the light was doing the same. The color was beautiful, such an incredible yellow. A great calm and euphoric joy came upon me, a wonderful sense that all was well. I understood that I was on my way to heaven. The yellow, the peace, the calm, all was so serene. What beauty. No pain, no stress, no worries at all.

"All at once...I saw a bright light from heaven shining around me." (Paul's life-changing moment on the Damascus Road, Acts 22:6 NIV)

The next thing I knew, I was in the back seat of a rental car, throwing up into the foot well. Sea water, it seemed like gallons of the stuff. I hauled myself up to see my friend, driving like a mad man on the wrong side of the road, heading straight for a green and beige Maltese bus. Was I going to die in a head-on collision? I passed out again.

Next, I remember being dragged out by my feet and put on a hospital gurney. I heard a loud noise and much wind. A helicopter stood by to fly me to Valetta, where a decompression chamber awaited.

It was determined that I did not have the bends or an embolism, which was a miracle in itself. After being pressurized at seventy-five feet, bubbles can form in the blood, which, if not treated in a hyperbaric chamber, can cause death.

I was to spend the next three days in the Royal Navy Hospital, with bandages on my feet, knees, elbows, and over a large gash on my head. I looked like an Egyptian mummy. Right away, I got the nickname, Mummy Mumford.

Looking back, I recall that I was actually not quite happy to have come back. I found myself a bit angry with the men who saved me! Later, I learned the story of my rescue. A Royal Navy dive team was at the Blue Grotto a few rocks away from where I was trying to climb out of the sea. They heard my shouts for help. One lad dove in and managed with the others to pull my lifeless body out of the water. Then they resuscitated me. I never met any of those lads, but whoever you are, thank you so very much for saving my life.

It took many sessions for a medic to remove forty sea urchin barbs from my feet, a few each day, without anesthetic. It was a painstaking and painful process. But I was alive, on sick duty, and walking around the base dressed like a mummy.

I was delivered, just like St. Paul after his shipwreck, on the rocky shore of Malta.

> "Once safely on shore, we found out that the
> island was called Malta." (Acts 28:1 NIV)

CHAPTER TWO

Gifts of the Spirit

AFTER THE DIVING accident, I told no one of my near–death experience, of my life review, or of the brilliant yellow tunnel. I kept it to myself for years, a weird phenomenon I thought no one would understand.

I left the Royal Marines after seven years and emigrated to the USA in 1980, opening a framing business in Connecticut. It was there I saw a TV program on near–death experiences. On the screen, right in front of my eyes, was a depiction of the yellow tunnel, illustrating what another drowning victim had encountered.

My call to the healing ministry came in 1989, shortly after my sister, Julie Sheldon, formerly a ballet dancer with the London Royal Ballet, was healed from dystonia, a severely crippling disease. Through the prayers of an Anglican priest, Canon Jim Glennon, and by the grace of God, she was completely cured.

Witnessing her healing, I was changed. Until then, I'd had no firsthand encounter with the gifts of the Spirit, as described in 1 Corinthians. It transformed my life completely.

"There are different kinds of service, but the same Lord.... Now to each one the manifestation of the Spirit is given for the common good. To one there is given through the Spirit a message of wisdom, to another a message of knowledge by means of the same Spirit, to another faith by the same Spirit, to another gifts of healing by that one Spirit, to another miraculous powers, to another prophecy, to another distinguishing between spirits, to another speaking in different kinds of tongues, and to still another the interpretation of tongues." (1 Cor.12: 5-10 NIV)

Soon after Julie's healing, I committed myself to the Christian healing ministry. The first appearances of the Spirit's healing gift within me took place in the unlikely setting of my frame shop! Five years later, I became a lay minister in the Episcopal Church. I had morphed from a Royal Marine to a healing minister! Canon Glennon became one of my mentors. He encouraged and empowered me until the day he died—June 11, 2005, the day I was ordained a deacon. Later that year, I was ordained a priest.

NEW YORK CITY, 2001

The destruction of the Twin Towers had a most profound effect on me. A month later, I found myself at "The Pile," ground zero, alongside those who were suffering loss, trying to find bodies in the rubble, sorting through tragedy. St. Paul's Chapel, neighboring the Towers, was covered in several feet of concrete dust but undamaged. The windows weren't even broken. I stood in the back of the church with a twenty-four-year-old volunteer, looking out the window at the still–smoking pile as she poured her heart out to me. It was her first time to debrief her experience of the horrors. At one point in our conversation, we opened the window. The smell that hit us was like a wall— a raw stench of concrete dust and rotting human flesh.

I had parked several blocks away, but even so, when I got in my car the next day and turned on the air conditioning, I was blasted again with that smell of concrete dust and death. I had to pull off the road to collect myself.

While I was at St. Paul's, my combat trauma and PTSD became sources I could draw upon to help others. I had been through the horrors of combat and the terror of near–dying in the diving accident. I'd also lived through the aftermath of those horrors, my mind wrestling with the impact of overwhelming stress.

Often our reaction to nearly losing our lives or witnessing others' loss of life is a shattering of our illusion of invincibility. We realize that we will not live forever. And when we come face–to–face with something like the Twin Towers, we encounter man's inhumanity to man. What do we do with such an overload of stimuli? The brain cannot sort it out. When we can't cope, the stress morphs into a physical reaction. The result can be PTSD.

In other words, PTSD is a normal reaction to an

abnormal situation. I've written more of this in *After the Trauma the Battle Begins: Post Trauma Healing*.

At ground zero, I discovered those experiences had equipped me to connect with people enduring trauma and to accompany them in their suffering, saying, "I know. I understand. I have crawled through the valley of death; I am right next to you." God had changed my combat trauma into a healing channel.

Now I know why the Lord pulled me out of that drowning. Mummy Mumford, you have work to do!

Chapter Three

Climbing the Cross

Greenville, South Carolina September, 2009

I WAS PREPARING to speak to a large audience at the First Presbyterian Church. In an office above the gathering, I was on my knees in prayer.

Immediately, I saw a vision of Christ on the Cross, His head lowered, His eyes fixed on me. It was as if He was telling me to pick up the ladder lying a few feet from the Cross. I told Him that the guards would stop me. He told me they would not. I did as I was asked, placing the top of the ladder just behind His left shoulder at the intersection of the two beams. Slowly, I climbed the ladder, wondering what I would experience—the flies, the smell, the blood? Here I was, worried about myself in the presence of Christ on the Cross. He was looking at me all the way up the ladder. I got level with His face. Jesus told me to put my right shoulder into His left shoulder. He told me in a whisper of gasping breath to lift him up. "I need to breathe," He said.

Gently I pushed Him up, my face almost touching His. He then looked out from the Cross and said in my right ear, "I want you to see what I see." I looked intently at the view from the Cross. I looked at the topography, I looked at the land.

Most paintings of the Lord on the Cross are focused on Him. I didn't recall any painting of what the Lord would have seen.

As fast as the vision had started, it stopped. I was still on my knees in the pastor's office. Someone came to tell me that the program was about to begin downstairs. I was escorted to a large room filled with people. The "happy-clappy" music of praise and worship began. It was beautiful.

Good worship music is so important during a healing conference. Like a large classical orchestra tuning up before a concert, we tune into God as the body of Christ. The music ended, and I was introduced. I said a prayer, walked away from the podium, and began to describe what had happened while I was praying in the pastor's office.

When I got to the part when Jesus said, "I want you to see what I see," I understood that He didn't mean the landscape. He wanted me to see the raw pain of the human condition in each person. His sentence was unfinished. If I were to fill in the rest of those powerful words, it would be, "I want you to see what I see in everyone I look at. I want you to see the fear, anxiety, worry, the pain, the hurt, the dis-ease, the rejection, the generational issues, the brokenness, the broken heart, the doubt, the faith, the love, the joy; I want you to see each person you look at with your soul. See the issue that person is carrying. As you see it, help them unpack it." I stood in silence as the revelation hit me, right in front of all those people. There was a long period of silence as I looked at each person with that intent to see. To really see what He sees. The power of the presence of the Holy Spirit alighted upon us all. It was a very powerful day of healing.

Later, Kathy DeLair, an artist friend, painted what I saw. My right shoulder was under the Lord's. She painted Christ upon the Cross as if my head were right next to His, in monochromatic stillness, with one drop of red blood falling from His forehead, His hair blowing forward in the storm, and the last vapor of the last breath coming from His mouth.

Looking back on this vision, I understood its full meaning. I saw that I/we must look at everyone through His eyes to fully understand the plight of the human condition.

I also saw how it spoke to me of events yet to come.

"Breathe on me, breath of God,

So shall I never die,

But live with Thee the perfect life

Of Thine eternity."[1]

---

[1] (*The Hymnal 1982*, Hymn 508, v. 4. Hatch, Edwin and Peace, Lister R. New York: Church Hymnal Group, 1985.

CHAPTER FOUR

The Battle Begins

IN SEPTEMBER, 2009, THE Royal Air Force invited me to fly to England and speak to military personnel about Post-Traumatic Stress. It was during the H1N1 swine flu pandemic. Many people at Heathrow airport were wearing white facemasks. I took on the bravado of, "Oh, that won't happen to me. I'm not wearing a facemask. I'm not even going to get the shot."

The weekend was a highlight for me, a time to converse about the stresses and strains put upon the military. While at the conference, I met the Chief of Staff of the British Armed forces, the Lord Richard Dannatt. I confess that I was nervous about meeting him. The highest rank I had spoken to while a Marine was Lt. Colonel, and here, right in front of me, was the highest–ranking man of the British Armed Forces!

When I was introduced, the General tilted his head forward, looked at me from under his eyebrows, and said, "Nigel, I report to God, the Queen, the Prime Minister, and my wife— in that order." There was a long pause. His face froze, awaiting my reply. My whole body locked up as I tried to say something. "How do you do?" seemed so lame a reply to such a statement. After what seemed an age, I thrust my right hand forward and said, "Sir, I like you."

The weekend went well. We delved into the intricacies of combat fatigue, trying to unpack how the mind and body react to horrific input. We recalled that the ancient Greeks suffered the aftereffects of war. Their mothers, wives, and girlfriends noticed how each man was different upon his return. It was a privilege to be one of the speakers at this conference. Could I have come in contact with the H1N1 during my visit to England or the airport?

I returned home from England in late September, where Lynn and I spent a few days in New York City to celebrate our eighth wedding anniversary. Within the week, I then few to Jacksonville, FL. Judith and Francis MacNutt, had invited me to be one of the speakers for the filming of in their advanced training class. I spoke on the issues of trauma both civilian and military life. There was a large audience in attendance.

When I had arrived at the hotel, my room seemed damp and musty. The air-conditioning filter, looked like it hadn't been cleaned in years! In hindsight, I should have asked for another room. I didn't want to make a fuss and slept in that room for 4 days! After finishing my talk, I had developed a cough, that seem to progress into the following day. By the time I flew home, to Greenwich, NY, the cough was getting worse. I arrive home on Friday, around midnight. That Saturday morning I woke up around 5:30am and began coughing. Lynn instinctively knew the cough was not normal, and suggested, since it's early, and it was holiday weekend (Columbus Day), let's go to the ER and get checked out.

I was seen fairly quickly, as it was quiet in the ER. After a body inspection, the doctor told me I had adult-onset asthma. He gave me a breathing treatment and an inhaler and sent me home. Lynn and I had a nice breakfast in a diner near the hospital and then drove home. Two hours later, the coughing resumed. I used the inhaler, collapsed, and lay on the floor covered in sweat. I could not breathe. I felt like a fish out of the tank, flopping around on the living room floor, gasping for air. I was in respiratory arrest.

Lynn dialed 911.

The ambulance arrived very quickly. They gave me another breathing treatment, strapped me to a gurney, and headed for Saratoga Springs Hospital.

The same doctor who had discharged me three hours before greeted me. The look on his face was a look I shall never forget. The honest look of "OMG! I've made a huge mistake," the realization that perhaps he should not have sent me home. I was given oxygen and admitted to the hospital for observation.

Much later, I wrote to that doctor telling him my side of the story and forgiving him. The look of sadness on his face was etched in my mind as I wrote the letter. That look of horror and surprise is a still photo in my memory, a sad

Kodak moment.

I was to spend the next six days in a hospital room, coughing. I had a barrage of tests and lung X–rays every day. At 4:15 a.m. each day, I was awakened by someone to take yet more blood. The words "Legionnaires' Disease" were thrown about. I don't have much memory of this incubation time, while the swine flu H1N1 was festering in my lungs.

The last thing I remember is being wheeled upstairs to ICU Room One. I'd been coughing a heavy, deep, gasping–for–air cough, so much that I was not sleeping at all. Now I was totally exhausted. The doctors recommended I be put into a coma while my body fought the infection. I remember looking at Lynn and saying, "I'm really frightened." She was asked to leave the room and was told, "He won't remember any of this."

I was in a coma for the next nineteen days.

It must have been awful for my bride. I found out later that she was by my bed from 8 a.m. to 8 p.m. every day for seventy-two days straight. What an amazing woman. I know my brother Alec came over from the UK twice while I was in the coma. He told me he poked my ankles and told me to get up, but I ignored him. I've seen photos of myself in a coma; it really looked like I was dead. My fingers, legs, and toes were swollen from steroids; my eyes were closed; and tubes were down my throat. Wires and ports were all over the place. I was totally plugged in and surrounded by life–sustaining equipment, angels, archangels, the whole company of heaven, and the prayers of the people. Thank you, God, for technology and for those gifted in using these machines.

I was out of my body, traveling—mostly to heaven. I began to have visions. The visions—so Biblical, so real, so poignant, so mine—were as if they really happened. In my mind, they did. These were different from dreams. There was more color, more detail, more of everything in life. I am glad I can remember the visions and not the extreme medical protocols that took place to save my life: insertion of a feeding tube; puncture of the collapsed lung; the tracheotomy.

Chapter Five

Visions

"'In the last days,' God says, 'I will pour out my Spirit on all people. Your sons and daughters will prophesy, your young men will see visions, your old men will dream dreams.'" (Acts 2:17 NIV)

Vision One: *Revelation*

The Living Waters

"...He will lead them to springs of living water. And God will wipe away every tear from their eyes." (Rev. 7:17 NIV)

The first vision was a single blade of grass. So green, so perfect, so lovely. It seemed that I looked at that blade of grass forever. After all, I had forever to look at it. I was surprised about its beauty and texture, its form and exquisite detail. I was focused on that single blade of grass with no distractions whatsoever. It was a perfect blade of grass, the perfect introduction to heaven. I looked at that single blade of grass for a long time. I saw its beauty, the color, the texture. Then, as if on a movie screen, the lens pulled back to reveal more and more blades of grass, all perfect, all different. All perfectly still. The perfection of God upon each of His creation. Was I actually looking at thousands of blades of grass or thousands of souls? I don't know.

I then saw three white tulips in a well-manicured garden. The soil around it was groomed to perfection, with not one speck of soil out of place. I looked; I observed. Was I looking at the Trinity? Was that God, Jesus, and the Holy Spirit? All was quiet; there was no sound. Pure silence. The perfect petals of the tulips were exquisite. Sadly, I have no recall of the sense of smell—just absolute beauty in a blade of grass, in the raised arms of the blades of grass and the three white tulips, the grass praising God, and heaven and nature praising the glory of the Lord.

Then the lens pulled back again, widening to reveal three granite steps, perfect in every way, the perfection of the Kingdom. The sun was bright. I looked, and I saw a path. There was my house. It was made of glass, held together by fire-engine-red angle irons. The red was brilliant, the glass clean and perfect.

The house was formed like a diamond; that is, the walls were not vertical. The bottom and the top of the house were V–shaped. I walked on a glass floor. There was no kitchen.

Instead, each room had a hole in the floor where a golden chalice hung from a golden chain. I bent down, grasped the golden chalice, and scooped up the living water that ran slowly through the house. It was the most delicious meal I have ever tasted.

Vision Two: *Hope*

<small>THE BOOK OF LIFE</small>

> "Another book was opened, which is
> the book of life." (Rev. 20:12 NIV)

It was dark, very dark. I was incredibly peaceful and reclined on a zero-gravity chair position in a hospital bed. The next thing I knew, I was rising up off the bed. I don't remember the ceiling; I just went up in the night air. I did not feel anything touching me. It just felt normal, no stress; actually, it was a good feeling. It just felt normal. Then I looked, and I saw the stars. It was all so clear. The dark was very dark; the individual stars, in contrast, were very bright indeed. I continued to be raised up now in slow motion as I took in the amazing view. Then I stopped and just floated miles above the earth.

I remember trying to turn my head to the left and realizing my head was being blocked. It was as if I was not allowed to look back. "That is the past; this is the now. You have no need to look back. No time for goodbyes." So I just looked up and out.

Then I saw a horizontal bar appear a long way off. It moved from the center, growing out for about a mile. Then it continued straight up on both sides, rising up for about six miles. Then the lines stopped and traveled towards each other. They connected, and the stars then formed in perfect lines, each one a brilliant light, almost too bright to look at. Still, I kept looking in awe and wonder. What was this? I did not understand at first, but I knew I was supposed to see it.

I looked into each light, not really knowing what it was. Then I understood it was the book of life. Each light was a soul. I looked below each light, expecting to see the details of each soul. I thought it would be like a huge scrapbook with the details posted in a little sign under each person. Not so. I had to look into each light to meet that soul and to see that person's history. I just had to look to understand. I felt I was being introduced to the whole company of heaven by being shown the book of life.

As I read, the pages turned from the bottom right corner slowly, like a huge sail. I could feel the wind as each page moved. I could not see the left page, but I looked at each light on the righthand page. I looked at those pages for a very long time—page after page of souls, all written in the book of life. I just lay there in the anti-gravity position, looking. I was neither hot nor cold nor hungry. I just met each soul, thousands on each page. Then the page would turn again. I must have seen millions and millions of souls.

Vision Three: *Perseverance*

THE VALLEY OF THE SHADOW OF DEATH

"Even though I walk through the darkest valley, I will fear no evil, for you are with me." (Ps. 23:4 NIV)

I was aware that I was crawling, using my elbows to pull myself along. I knew my legs were paralyzed. The white and pink polished marble path was slippery and worn. The air was musty. I was struggling and out of breath, but I knew I had to keep going. Looking left and right, I saw jagged rocks stacked up to the top of the valley. There was no way out. I knew I was in the valley of the shadow of death. I did not feel any fear. It felt normal, but I had to keep going. A Royal Marine, I had to persevere toward the goal, the goal of heaven's gate. Still, at this point I was very tired and started to despair.

I looked up to my right and saw the Lord Jesus Christ on the Cross. He was staring at me, His head slumped toward His right, His eyes perfectly fixed on me.

Jesus did not say anything, but pushed me on with His eyes. He moved His eyes in the direction I was going. He did not smile, but His eyes were compassionate. He seemed to be saying, "Nigel, you can do it. Press on." I kept crawling with my arms, keeping my eyes on the Lord. Then He was gone. I stopped and looked ahead. All appeared in shades of sepia brown. Even the marble path was looking brown.

Now He was on the left, another five hundred yards down the valley. I could see His eyes, still urging me on. This vision went on and on. First to the left, then to the right, Jesus would appear on the cross. He was in pain. His face was so very sad. His eyes were filled with love, compassion, encouragement.

I kept crawling. The valley now went slightly downward, meandering more and more. The brown shades were getting darker and darker. The colors were turning toward black.

I came to a halt. To my left was a sharp forty-five-degree turn. I looked down the valley and saw two dark pillars on either side of the path. They were smooth, compared to all the jagged angles around. They were so dark that they stood out in the darkness—such a deep black they gave the impression that they were not even solid, just a huge void.

Am I going to Hell after all of this? "No, no," I tried to scream. No noise came from me. Where Are You, God? Again, I looked ahead and saw the Lord, on the Cross, looking at me, but His eyes were filled with joy. He was saying, "This way, follow me." I was so relieved. I was not being led into Hell. He just wanted me to see the gates.

As I crawled on, it got lighter. On and on I went, following Jesus on the Cross. Then I saw it: about a hundred yards ahead where the valley opened up, two brilliant white pillars blazed with light. I did not see the gates; I think they must have been open. There was total silence. I stopped crawling to take in the bright shapes, strangely illuminated as if from within. There were no shadows and no noise. I could not see beyond the pillars, but I was very calm and ready to continue crawling to the pillars and through the gates. Then the vision ended.

"What is the way to the abode of light? And where does darkness reside? Have the gates of death been shown to you? Have you seen the gates of the deepest darkness?" (Job 38:16-19 NIV)

Vision Four: *Expectation*

A Table Before Me

> "Wait for the Lord; be strong and take heart
> and wait for the Lord." (Ps. 37:14 NIV)

I was sitting next to the head of the table, the carver's chair to my right. The table was not yet prepared. It looked like an English dining room in a castle, a long room with walnut paneling on the lower part of the walls and dark green wallpaper on the top. The table was of a dark walnut, with carved legs and carved chairs. Over my head was a cylinder, also covered in green wallpaper. I knew what was inside that cylinder— the relics of St. Therese of Lisieux. I had seen the same clear plastic cylinder in the Basilica at Lisieux. She prays for clergy. I knew Saint Therese was with me and praying for me. I found that very comforting, very peaceful.

For a long time, I sat and waited, just being. There was no rush, plenty of time. There was nowhere else I needed to be. A door was to my right. I knew what I was waiting for. The Lord would come through the door at any moment. I felt He was going to introduce Himself to me and give me a briefing as to the do's and don'ts of heaven! I sat and took in the view, observing everything in great detail. I was in the briefing room of heaven, waiting on the Lord. "Come on, Jesus! I'm so looking forward to this." I waited and waited. It was a long wait. I began to think I had been forgotten. He never came. I was deeply disappointed.

Vision Five: *Preparation*

In My Father's House Are Many Rooms

"Do not let your hearts be troubled. You believe in God; believe also in me. My Father's house has many rooms; if that were not so, would I have told you that I am going there to prepare a place for you? And if I go and prepare a place for you, I will come back and take you to be with me that you also may be where I am. You know the way to the place where I am going."
(John 14:1-4 NIV)

I was an observer, looking from above, as if from a helicopter. Below were many large houses, Victorian in style, painted all sorts of colors, with wraparound porches and filigree work. Many windows, many rooms—these were rooms indeed. All the gardens were well–manicured, nothing out of place. I saw large lakes with beautiful fountains, but no roads. The houses were connected with a small–gauge railway. A calm and a peace pervaded it all. I saw no one, but I imagined people traveling in the trains. Come to think of it, I didn't see any trains. It was all very serene, very welcoming. I found this deeply comforting.

"Lord, by such things people live; and my spirit finds life in them too. You restored me to health and let me live. Surely it was for my benefit that I suffered such anguish. In your love you kept me from the pit of destruction; you have put all my sins behind your back. For the grave cannot praise you, death cannot sing your praise; those who go down to the pit cannot hope for your faithfulness. The living, the living— they praise you, as I am doing today; parents tell their children about your faithfulness. The Lord will save me, and we will sing with stringed instruments all the days of our lives in the temple of the Lord."

–Hezekiah's prayer. (Is. 38:16-20 NIV)

Chapter Six

The Prayers of the People

"IS ANYONE AMONG you sick? Let them call the elders for the church to pray over them and anoint them with oil in the name of the Lord. And the prayer offered in faith will make the sick person well; the Lord will raise them up. If they have sinned, they will be forgiven." (James 5:14-15 NIV)

"I urge you, brothers and sisters, by our Lord Jesus Christ and by the love of the Spirit, to join me in my struggle by praying to God for me." (Rom. 15:30 NIV)

EVERY SINGLE DAY, for days on end, Beth Strickland, deployment officer for the diocese of Albany and a dear friend, updated those who were praying for me via the Internet. My wife, Lynn, was the first line of defense; then Sandra Lester, who supported Lynn through the ordeal;

and then Beth, who let people know how to pray for me as accurately as possible. (HIPAA[2] seemed pointless by then!)

Each day, Lynn and Sandra gathered as much information as possible from the doctors and nurses and described the prayer target to Beth, who then published the exact need. She gave people a target, a mission, and a focus: what to pray for and how to pray for the hourly or daily presenting issue.

Beth posted prayer instructions, such as, "Fr. Nigel needs prayer that his body temperature of 105 will decrease; that the ice blanket will help; that dialyses will chill the blood; that the sepsis will leave; that his organs, which are in total organ failure, will respond to prayer; that the carbon dioxide will leave his body as the oxygen pours into his lungs; and that the MRSA[3] infection from the (tracheotomy) will leave." The prayer request went out via the diocesan web page. Within days, thousands of people around the world were praying for me.

People would call or e-mail, saying they didn't know who this Nigel Mumford was, but they felt drawn to get on their knees to pray for him. Some people were saying that they had not been on their knees to pray in years, but were overwhelmed by the urge to pray and even the urge to kneel.

On the night of October 23, 2009, the doctors told Lynn, Sandra, and Beth that they had done all they could for me.

Beth said, "Good, now God will take over."

At the same time that evening, our friend Judith MacNutt heard the news that I had taken a turn for the

2[The Health Insurance Portability and Accountability Act of 1996, patient privacy of medical records legislation]

3 MRSA, a type of staph infection, is deadly because of its resistance to antibiotics.

worse. She was driving, and she pulled off the road to pray. To her companion, she said, "Nigel is dying."

God really did take over. The web exploded with prayer. A tsunami of prayer surged over me, an outpouring of power, glory, and praise. I am convinced that the prayer— the power of thousands praying all over the world— saved my life. How very humbling to be on the receiving end.

Many who prayed for me in that time of crisis have since shared their side of the story, saying how their faith was uplifted. Many came back to faith, and many returned to church. People knew how to pray and felt led to pray. At the time, I did nothing except receive.

So how do we pray for the sick? Gentle holy boldness and a quiet confidence are the nature of the prayer warrior, the intercessor, the secret weapon of the church.

If we are in the physical company of a sick person, we ask, "How may I pray for you?" We hear the history as we listen, love, and pray for them. We may pray in silence or pray into the history of the concerns that the supplicant has shared. (Please, let's avoid the word 'just,' as in, "Lord, just take away this disease!")

In our mind's eye, we see the target of prayer; we pour our words, thoughts, love, and Christian expression into the wound, be it physical, emotional, generational, or mental. We see the target—the cancer, the depression, the issue; and we literally pour our love and prayer into this dis-ease, "taking on to believe" for that person. Sometimes I see my prayer as a scalpel slicing into the disease.

How do we pray for someone who may be miles away? That is, how do we intercede or become an intercessor for a relative, a loved one, a friend, or even someone we don't know? Again, we gather as many facts as we can, we identify the target, and we pour our prayers into the disease by faith. I find the world wide web to be very helpful in finding the facts of the presenting problem, to get an understanding. Then I can pray into the issue with all my mind, heart, body, and soul.

"Pray for each other so that you may be healed. The prayer of a righteous person is powerful and effective." (James 5:16 NIV)

If you are called to pray for others, if you intercede on behalf of others, you—yes, you—are part of the backbone of faith. Well done, good and faithful servant, keep up the "God work." Keep praying in faith, keep believing.

"Cast your care on the Lord, and He will sustain you; He will never permit the righteous to be moved." (Ps.55:22 NIV)

Chapter Seven

The Killing Table

November 4, 2009

I'D BEEN "OUT" for nineteen days. My condition had improved enough for the medical team to plan to bring me back from the coma. But first, I'd have to be taken off the ventilator and given a tracheostomy (trach) tube to supplement my oxygen. A "trach" is a curved tube inserted through a hole made in the neck and windpipe, which serves as an airway.

They scheduled me for a tracheotomy on November 4. Bluntly put, this involves cutting the patient's throat and inserting a tube into the lungs.

Although I was still in a coma, I was somehow aware of these events!

My perception, distorted and dark, was drenched in fear:

I was being wheeled on a gurney to a green 'killing table.' I heard people talking and the clinking of champagne glasses. It was my funeral. There I saw my coffin, lid open, waiting for me. I heard people saying things you say at a funeral, but I couldn't make out the words. There seemed to be laughter and joy.

Then two male nurses lifted me from a gurney and threw me onto the killing table. It was a putrid light green color. The nurses held me down. One placed his knee on my throat. They were determined to close my windpipe. I thought I was in Sweden, where we were living when mandatory euthanasia was in place.

My funeral was to be at 10 a.m. I saw the clock. It was nine–thirty, and I was not dead yet. This was all rather Monty Python-esque! "I'm not dead yet," I wanted to declare. Then all went dark.

• • •

This nightmare haunted me. For several years, I didn't even talk about it. Not until I was writing about it for *After the Trauma, The Battle Begins* did I actually confront what had happened. I stopped writing. Something was terribly wrong. Then I asked Lynn what time the tracheotomy had been scheduled. She said, "Ten o'clock." It made sense.

Although I was in a coma, I heard sounds, felt hands touching me, knew I was being moved, and even knew what time it was—approaching ten o'clock. The talking I'd heard was conversation between the doctor and nurses prepping me for surgery. The clinking of champagne glasses was the sound of surgical tools being prepared. The knee on my throat was the surgeon's hand, and then the scalpel.

I have to say the memory of this trauma is not all healed. In fact, a good friend of mine, a former FBI agent, recently went to grab my throat in jest. I did not think; I just did an instinctive karate move with full contact—and nearly broke my friend's arm . . . A residual post–trauma response.

The tracheotomy was actually a positive step, removing me from the ventilator and allowing me to recover my own breathing ability. After the trach device in my throat was removed, gauze was placed over the hole. No stitches were needed. My throat made some very weird gurgling noises for a little while, and within half an hour, it was healed. The human body is just amazing.

Now I seem to have two Adam's apples, the real one, and the scar tissue one. My clergy collar covers up the wound. My mind tries to cover up the scar.

Chapter Eight

Recovery

"WHEN YOU WALK, they will guide you; when you sleep, they will watch over you; when you awake, they will speak to you." (Prov. 6:22 NIV)

"Then the angel who talked with me returned and woke me up, like someone awaked from sleep." (Zech. 4:1 NIV)

WAKING FROM THE coma took a week or more. The drip was stopped, and after a few hours, I am told, finally my eyes opened. The nurses said, "Oh, look! He has brown eyes." They were very excited. I'm told that I just stared, blank-eyed, unable to follow. Heads would move around, and I heard voices saying things to me. People moved in and out of my range like huge heads on tiny bodies. Faces would ask me to blink—once for yes, twice for no. I thought

I was already doing that.

I wondered, "Where did heaven go?"

"I'm not in the valley of the shadow of death anymore?"

"Where has my house in heaven gone?"

"Why are you all looking at me with such compassion?"

Then I'd sleep again. I slept a lot. Wake, then sleep again. Slowly things started to make sense. I thought I had been "out" for three hours. It was three weeks!

The first thing I remember understanding was that nothing on my body moved except my right index finger. I could move it up and down about half an inch. That was all. I had an itch, couldn't scratch it, and couldn't tell anyone about it. I was very calm and had no fear whatsoever about not moving. I just accepted it. But I was aware of agonizing pain in my lower spine—raw, unadulterated, never–ceasing, excruciating pain from a deep pressure sore. "You don't need to be in pain," I was told. Unable to talk, I couldn't describe the torment to anyone. Each nurse who came on duty asked me who I was, what my date of birth was, and what my pain level was. "What's your pain level on a scale of 1-10?"

I tried to say, "It's 110!"

Lynn told me later that the nurses, watching all the machinery dials measuring my body's condition, knew I was in pain. They would up my meds.

Many irrational fears percolated in my mind. I worried about someone walking off the street and coming into my room. It was terrifying, not being able to speak or to push the red 'Nurses' button. I hated the bed curtains being closed, fearing I would be forgotten. The curtains, set in place for privacy, were like a prison wall. They appeared to have little boxes sewn on them, each handmade, each different. I imagined these boxes were made of rusting steel, with hollow cut−out windows, each about half the size of a shoe box, each containing a prayer from someone intent on my demise.

"The enemy, the devil, prowls around like a lion waiting to devour." (1 Pet. 5–8 NIV)

As I later learned, at that time a friend of mine mentioned to a classmate that he was praying for me. The other person said, to my friend's horror, that he was a member of a coven and was praying that I would die. My friend looked at his former classmate in shock and horror and walked away without turning back.

This confirms to me that a battle was going on for my soul. Countering that battle were thousands of people around the world praying for my very life. The truth is that the Lord was watching over me during this battle for my soul.

I was not able to tell anyone about the boxes. I can recall them now, but wish I had been able to talk about them at the time. I realize that this dark time could have been a product of the many drugs I'd been given. The thought of those boxes evokes fear in me even now.

In prayer, I have placed the Lord Jesus between me and that horrible memory. Placing Jesus between me and the symbolic has helped me realize that the curtain was actually keeping evil out of my room, fighting the spirit of death.

As the Lord heals this memory, I see the Him standing in my room. With one swing of His arm, He sweeps those fetish boxes off the curtains. I can hear them hitting the polished floor, bouncing in slow motion. I see Him kicking them under the curtain, out of sight. Although the fear stays in my memory, it has no power. The power of God is far greater than the power of evil. The truth sets us free.

At first, I spent a lot of time just staring, wondering, "Who am I? What am I? Where am I?" (I have to say that the word "Why" never entered my mind, even today.) Coming back from heaven was taking a lot of time, most of it without my comprehension. I stared at anything my eyes rested on, with my brain in neutral, finding time for healing.

It was not until my stepdaughter, Megan, came into the room that I recognized someone. Then I knew who Lynn was—my poor bride, who had been sitting there from 8 a.m. to 8 p.m. for seventy-three days.

I remember my first words spoken through the trach. One word for one breath. Looking at Lynn, with a nurse in the room, I remember saying, "I." (Breath,) "Love." (Breath,) "You." (Breath.)

Tears came pouring down the respiratory nurse's face and, I confess, my face. I heard my strange voice coming from my trached throat and realized that I was alive.

One of the nurses who had been there from the beginning, Tasha, was amazed when she heard me. "I love the English accent!" she proclaimed.

Later, talking to the doctor, one word for one breath, I had to think about the words and force them out of my mouth via the trach: "Doc, will, l, be, able, to, play, the, piano, again."

He responded with a huge smile, "Oh, yes. I'm sure you will."

I responded, "Funny, that, I, could, not, play, it, before, I, was, sick."

It was time for me to brush my own teeth for the first time in months. Tooth brushing until now had been done by others, using a pad on the end of a stick. Most unpleasant. Now I was given a toothbrush with a huge foam handle. I'm left handed, but only the right side of my body could move. So I tried using my right hand to move my left arm around. It just would not move. My right hand grabbed my left wrist, but the fingers dropped limp. Next, I took the toothbrush in my right hand, toothpaste on the bristle. I missed my mouth completely and stuck the brush straight up my left nostril! I was so startled.

Looking back on it now, it's funny, but at the time, I was devastated. Here it was, time to get me doing basic personal stuff, a huge step forward, but I couldn't even brush my teeth! Getting dressed was equally stressful. I hated putting on tight T–shirts, which felt so claustrophobic. I couldn't breathe while I was moving my arms into the thing. Was this as well as I was going to get? Was this as good as my life would be? I remember feeling sorry for myself, thinking I would never be able to play the violin again. (How wrong was I in limiting the Lord?)

I struggled to understand what was happening. My brain just couldn't connect the dots. It was as if my mind were dulled by Novocain. Maybe that was a good thing, now that I look back on it. I was numb to what was actually going on, except for the physical pain. (Oh, no. It's 4:15 a.m. again. Time to hunt around with the needle to find blood in the collapsed vein!) Often, nurses would come in shouting.

Perhaps the last patient was deaf. I would answer quietly, saying, "My body is a mess, but I am not deaf!" This became a joke with many nurses.

Every time I sat up, I was nauseous. The physical therapy (PT) staff kept trying to get me to sit up. My inner ear seemed to have reset itself, or the drugs were still playing havoc. I was seasick. It brought back memories of being in a force 7 gale in the North Sea in a 55-foot sailboat, clinging to the rail and feeling so bad; of crossing the Bay of Biscay, off the west coast of Spain, in a force 8 storm; of washing dishes on an aircraft carrier, rushing to the rail—not so fond memories of seasickness. I thought I would never be upright again. This was it; this was how I would spend the rest of my life, lying on a gurney.

They gave me seasick pills; they worked.

By the first week of December, I had improved enough to be transferred to Sunnyview Rehab Hospital. I'd had to really prove myself, to try as hard as I could to get my body working again, to qualify. Moving to rehab was the carrot dangled in front of me. It was like being back in the Marines.

I remember saying goodbye to all the nurses in ICU and being wheeled in the gurney, with all the lights in the ceiling clearing in my eyes. We had a little procession toward the door where the ambulance was waiting for me. Then, a moment of freedom. Sunlight, fresh chilly air—finally, I was out of the hospital!

Where had the leaves gone? When I went in, it was October. Now the trees were bare! Where did those three months go? I'm alive . . . I'm alive . . . Oh what a feeling. If I could have, I would have jumped off the gurney. On the one hand, I was exhilarated. On the other, I was terrified, leaving the safe and familiar. Now everything would change. Breathe, I told myself. Keep breathing. Smile. Know this is a huge step in the right direction.

The journey seemed to last forever. Then I was wheeled into my new digs—different faces, some smiling, some really stressed out.

I would adapt to my new surroundings.

PT was very strict with me. I felt like a recruit in the Royal Marines. This time, beautiful female drill sergeants were telling me I had to do stuff I really did not want to do. What a nightmare it must have been, trying to get me to live again! "Keep breathing," I would hear. "Smell the roses. Blow out the candles."

I wanted to shout, "Leave me alone." But I could only whisper and try to smile. To this day, I have to remember to be aware of my breathing. Lynn tells me sometimes I still breathe in the same way as the machine that kept me alive—a short power breath and then nothing. They say we have muscle memory; this type of breathing certainly confirms that.

Rehab became a daily routine. The morning started at 4:15 a.m. with a blood test, the lights full on, a shouting phlebotomist poking the needle around in my arm, trying to find a vein. I would snooze for a while. Then I would be washed, and PT would come and dress me, teaching me what to do. I should know how to do this, but not with this body! We had to get creative. It was such hard work.

Then I would be wheeled to the exercise area. I'd spend twenty minutes on the hand bike. Many times PT tried to get me to sit on the recumbent bikes, but the intense pain of the bed sore did not allow that.

Bit by bit, day by day, I improved. I so looked forward to the weekends! I was missing Lynn, as she now could come to visit me only in the afternoons.

I found myself just staring at the second hand of the wall clock. Then someone would shout, "Smell the roses. Blow out the candles." These became words I heard a hundred times a day. They became triggers for me. When at last I could talk, I had to tell the nurses and occupational therapists (OTs), "Please . . . I can't hear that anymore!"

Lynn and I now have an agreement not to say "Smell the roses. Blow out the candles." These words are banned from our home.

When would this nightmare end? It seemed I had forgotten how to breathe.

Reflecting on life's basic needs makes me realize how much we take for granted. Slowly, very slowly, my body and mind began to work again. I do confess that the sessions to get me walking were frightening. Hanging on for dear life to the two-wheeled walker with tennis balls on the back legs, I had a belt around my waist, a PT person beside me, and another with a hand around a tight strap around my waist. I had to find the muscles to make my legs move and, at the same time, remember to breathe. I was doing the Tim Conway shuffle.

My drill instructor days flashed back. "You're moving like a handcuffed crab, laddie." Or, "Noooo! Move your left arm as you move your right leg." Or, "It's mind over matter, lad; I don't mind, and you don't matter." I entertained myself when there was no pain. I tried to be as nice as I could to everyone, but pain often won. I tried to smile and hide the tears leaking out of my eyes.

I didn't know how to pray, was off-the-charts depressed, in massive pain, and struggling. I was totally reliant on others praying for me. "Where are you, God?"

Little by little, my body relearned what it was supposed to do. I was being rewired after completely blowing all my circuits. Control, Alt, Delete . . . Reboot. It was exhausting work. Looking back now, it makes sense, but at the time, I thought that this was as good as it was going to get. I asked people about the future, but just kept getting vague phrases of encouragement. Several people visited and helped me try to make sense of it all. Some deep conversations with my bride and visiting clergy about the Bible and my trips to heaven helped a lot.

I vividly remember the doctor telling me what was wrong with me and my reaction in breaking down. I had feared that it was H1N1 swine flu before, and now it was confirmed. Later, I was told about a man ten years younger, admitted to the hospital four months after me, who did not make it. My heart was broken for him and his family.

The first time I saw myself in the mirror, I thought, "Who is that looking at me?" I thought I was seeing a corpse. Or a concentration camp survivor, sunken eyes, hollow cheeks, and lost. It was such a shock. My face had caved in. I'd lost so much weight, I looked like a dead man walking. It was all I could do to stand up, with the thick belt around my waist, held by the PT person behind me.

Now I tell people that I lost 68 pounds on the swine flu diet, but have put on 72 pounds since. "Eat bacon" someone suggested, "and get your revenge."

CHAPTER 9

Trust: the Primary Caregiver's View

A Reflection by Nigel's wife, Lynn Mumford

I write this chapter as a testimony of the healing grace of our Lord, Jesus Christ.

"The Lord is my strength and my shield; my heart trusts in Him, and He helps me. My heart leaps for joy, and with my song I praise Him." (Ps. 28:7 NIV)

THE WORD "TRUST" has been a message from God to Nigel and me. It started early in our relationship. A local newspaper did a story about a prayer walk Nigel had created. A reporter took a photo of Nigel speaking to me, my back to the camera. When the picture appeared in the paper, it showed, nailed to a tree above our heads, a sign with the word "Trust." Little did we know then that this would echo constantly in our lives: Trust—in Him.

> "Commit your way to the Lord; trust in Him
> and He will do this." (Ps. 37:5 NIV)

In the fall of 2009, I asked Jesus to please heal my husband. "Don't let him die," I prayed. I promised God that if He would cure him, I would stand and testify of God's healing grace and that miracles do happen! I'm sure many of you have also negotiated with the Lord, making promises or "deals," such as if He does this, I will do that.

I believed that once I gave my testimony, I would have fulfilled my promise to God. No way! Next time you make a promise to God, take note of the "fine print." This will not be a one-time moment! I have been led to give my testimony over ten times.

As an introvert, I find it is not easy to stand on stage before a crowd of people and give testimony of how the Lord healed and saved my husband's life. Many times, I've thought, "I don't want to talk about it anymore! I don't want to relive it! The past is the past; let's move on." But the Lord keeps reminding me, "This was our agreement."

People still ask me, "What was it like to watch your husband in the ICU, not knowing if he would survive?" Even when Nigel asked me to write this chapter, I procrastinated. Then I remembered my agreement with the Lord: "Tell them!" I hope my story helps you when life throws you a curve ball you didn't expect.

By the time you get to this chapter, you'll know what happened to Nigel. Here are some of my own recollections.

On Saturday, October 9, when Nigel was first admitted to the hospital, I was not too concerned. I knew he was in good hands with the hospital staff. Saturday, Sunday, Monday, I saw that Nigel seemed to be getting worse, not better. By the evening of Wednesday, October 13, four days after being admitted, Nigel was running a low-grade fever. The nurse noticed pneumonia in his lungs. His oxygen treatment was increased from 20% to 60%.

The next morning, Thursday, I found Nigel in another room, with the ventilator supplying 100% of his oxygen. He barely could stay awake. The cough was chronic, and he was exhausted. My fears amplified. "Why, Lord?" I asked, "What is happening?" By 11 a.m. that day, Nigel was moved to ICU.

Friday, October 15, I arrived at the hospital around 8:30 a.m. I remember climbing the stairs to the ICU on the second floor. (It was my new routine, to keep fit and not use the elevator.) On the staircase, I met one of Nigel's pulmonologists. I asked, "How is Nigel?" and he said, "He is not doing well."

When I entered the ICU, Nigel's other pulmonologist was waiting for me. He took me aside for privacy and said that Nigel had had a difficult night. "He is exhausted from coughing," the doctor told me. "We are going to give him a chemical that will put him into a deep sleep, a chemical-induced coma. We'll have the machine breathe for him to give his body a chance to rest. At the same time, we'll give him a paralyzing medicine to relax the lungs and prevent reflux. This paralyzing med is only to calm the lungs."

He went on, "Now, Nigel will not remember any of

this. The time will be completely gone from his memory. Unfortunately, you will remember everything."

He asked for my consent. There was no question that this was the best and only option.

I remember being upset. The doctor was kind, asking if I had family to come be with me. I don't know why, but I told him I had no family, that Nigel was all I had. (My family was out of state, and my mother, the person I would have wanted, had died eight years earlier. Nigel's family was in the UK. I felt alone, at that very moment . . . but I was never alone when I look back!)

I had five minutes to visit with Nigel before they put him into the coma. It was now 9 a.m.

I went into Nigel's ICU room. He was so exhausted. They must have told him what they were going to do, because he seemed frightened. In fact, he told me so, breathlessly. I was upset, but I told Nigel he would be fine. Not to worry. Nigel insisted I talk with the hospital chaplain, a good friend of ours who had been checking on Nigel at the time. Nigel wanted me to say I would, and I agreed. I was quickly whisked away as they prepared to induce the coma. (Chaplain Rich Hoffman was very kind, checking with me throughout our hospital stay.)

After about thirty minutes in the family waiting room outside of ICU, I was able to go back into Nigel's room. The tube down his throat was taped to his mouth, a drip was hooked up, and the sound of a ventilator filled the room. Knowing this machine was breathing for him, it didn't frighten me. I knew how hard Nigel had been struggling to breathe. He was getting 100% oxygen from the ventilator, but his blood oxygen level reading was only 92. If he was turned onto his side for bathing or changing of bed sheets, his blood oxygen level would drop to 86, and an alarm would sound! After these ordeals, I would sit and watch, praying for the oxygen level to climb back up . . . 87, 88, 90, 91 . . .

The Very Rev. Dave Bena and his wife Mary Ellen were the first to come to the ICU that morning. They were a comfort to me. My daughter Megan and Sandra Lester arrived later in the morning. I believe I had texted them the latest update when Nigel was being put in an induced coma.

Megan stayed at my side along with my dear friend and soul sister, Sandra. What we thought would be two to four days in a coma on a ventilator ended up to be over nineteen days. The Lord provided me with close and dear friends to help me through this time. (I was not alone.)

Sandra talked with the doctors and nurses, asking all the necessary questions, since I was in shock and too emotional to think clearly. Our friend Beth Strickland made it her priority to see that I was never alone at the hospital. She would bring her laptop to the ICU waiting room, keeping the diocesan "blog" updated so everyone would know how to pray for Nigel. Since my husband was well-known and loved by many, this was personal for me, and I had requested no visitors at the hospital. He was mine, and I was not sharing.

Two days after Nigel was put on the ventilator and in an induced coma, his brother Alec flew over from England. I had been on the phone constantly with Nigel's family, keeping them informed. Eventually, Sandra took over this role for me. (She actually took over my cell phone, since I did not want to speak to anyone.)

Alec was able to speak directly to the doctors and nurses, to see what an outstanding facility the Saratoga Hospital ICU is, and to convey this information directly to the family in England. Having Alec by my side was such a comfort. He could only stay three days, but promised me he would come back the following week. I didn't want him to leave.

We'd thought Nigel would be in the coma for only a few days, but there was no improvement. I remember my thoughts and questions to God.

"Why?" I asked. "Is my husband going to die? Why are You only giving us eight years of marriage? Why would you take him, when he is doing Your work, Lord—praying for and healing the sick? It does not make sense. This is not of You, Lord! Fix it, please!"

During the coma, I would sit by Nigel's bed and rub his fingers and hands to help reduce the swelling. (Steroids had made his legs, feet, and hands very swollen.) When the nurse gave me his wedding ring. I put it on my necklace chain with the cross I was wearing and never took off during his stay in the hospital and rehab. I placed a prayer blanket over his feet and stroked his hair, since he used to like that. I spoke to him at times, telling him to get better. I told Nigel his brother Alec was coming from England to visit. While Alec was visiting, we told Nigel how rude it was to not to speak to him, when he came all that way! (I must say, humor from family and friends is so helpful.)

All prayer was welcomed. Some friends would come and read scripture; some would just chat and tell him they were waiting for him to wake up, etc. At times, a few of us would have Holy Communion around his bedside, reciting the words out loud, hoping Nigel would hear those word he knew by heart, "This is my body, which has been given for you…"

> "Truly I tell you, if you have faith as small as
> a mustard seed, you can say to this mountain, 'Move
> from here to there,' and it will move. Nothing will
> be impossible for you." (Matt. 17:20 NIV)

I decided to change my prayers, to stop asking God to heal my husband completely, asking instead for "mustard seeds" of healing: "Just show me some positive signs that Nigel is, and will get, better!" As small as one mustard seed may be, when you add each healing seed, the healing grows bigger and bigger.

Throughout this book you have heard the details of Nigel's illness. I can now look back to the turning point of his healing. It was Friday, October 23, fourteen days after he was admitted to the hospital. By now, Nigel was near death. He had developed secondary pneumonia on top of the pneumonia he already had. He had a fever of 105 degrees, his liver and kidneys had shut down, and he was on 100% ventilator oxygen.

That evening, around 5 p.m., Nigel's doctor pulled me aside and said, "There is nothing more they can do."

How can a healthy 55-year-old man so suddenly be at death's door?

Prayer vigils were held in the hospital lobby and the ICU waiting room. The nurses put an ice blanket over him, as well as ice packs under his armpits and knees to keep the fever down. I remember yelling into Nigel's ear, "You can't leave me! You can't die!"

During those days at the hospital, Megan, Sandra, and I camped in the ICU waiting room. On occasion, we were asked to move to the outside hall waiting room so the family of a dying patient could gather there. When this happened, the hospitality department of the hospital would bring an overflowing food cart to the ICU waiting room for the family.

That night, October 23, the food cart was brought to the waiting room for us.

We slept in the ICU waiting room. The next day, Saturday, there was no change in Nigel's condition. Megan and I agreed to stay another night in the hospital. Early Sunday morning, October 25, around 3 a.m., I walked into Nigel's room and saw that the ice blanket and ice packs had been removed. Nigel's fever was down to 102. "It's a start! A mustard seed!"

On Monday, the doctors told me Nigel's liver was back to normal. The kidneys were not yet working, but they should return to normal as his lungs recovered. Nigel was still in critical condition, but I was seeing those mustard seeds accumulating.

That evening, his 'port' was moved to the upper right chest; Nigel's right lung collapsed. Rare, but not unheard of when placing a port in that area. Immediately, a tube to inflate the lung was placed in his right side. It was a five-minute procedure. The tube pierced the lung and drained a lot of fluid from his right lobe. His blood oxygen level began to go up. Another mustard seed! A negative that actually was a positive!

The improved blood oxygen level meant Nigel could be weaned from the ventilator. If his dependence on ventilated oxygen could be lessened from 100% to around 60%, a tracheotomy could be performed, and the chemical drip that kept him in a coma could be stopped.

That week, Nigel had dialysis three or four times. His fever went down, and his kidneys went back to normal function. At week's end, Nigel was now on only 70% supplemental ventilated oxygen. A date was set for the tracheotomy–November 4.

My son Matt had flown in from California just to check on me. He could stay for only two days, but it was a comfort to have him close by. We were able to celebrate a bit since Nigel had begun to show improvement.

On October 31, Halloween, Nigel was doing fine, but his heart rate was very high. The rhythm was up and down, and the nurses were trying to regulate him. His blood oxygen level was still good, but Nigel's stats were crazy— almost like high adrenaline. (Remember, it was Halloween!)

On Sunday, November 1, All Saints' Day, the nurses were thrilled. His stats were perfect! He was calm, heart rate was normal, blood oxygen was 96! Nigel was still on schedule to have the trach.

He was now on only 60% oxygen supplemented by the ventilator.

Wednesday, November 4th, I couldn't wait! It was almost a celebration. The tracheotomy was to be done at 10 a.m. in his hospital room. The nurses had prepped everything for the doctor, who happened to be running late. The procedure took ten minutes or less.

When I was able to go back into Nigel's room, it was nice not to have the tube in his mouth. He now had the tube at his neck. The ventilator continued, but now he was being weaned from it. Nigel began to open his eyes.

It was nice to see those brown eyes again! He would open and close his eyes. He was still dreaming. I was told it would take almost five days for the drugs to leave his body. Sometimes he gave me strange looks when I came into his room during that time . . . Those drug-induced dreams were frightening!

Slowly, he awakened, began to think more clearly, and struggled to regain his strength. Healing was taking place.

Nigel had to meet certain requirements from PT in the ICU to qualify for the rehab facility. One goal was to walk at least six steps from the door of his room to his bed. Being nauseous and in pain made it so difficult for him— but this is a Marine! I watched and cheered! Nigel met the qualifications and was accepted.

Transfer was scheduled for December third. When they moved his gurney to the exit area, Nigel had his first taste of fresh air in two months. He was thrilled to feel the sunshine. Luckily it was a mild winter day. They put him in a medical transport van, and Megan and I followed in our car. It was about a forty-minute ride. Then there was the admitting process and getting him to his room—a very tiring day, but a significant step on his road to recovery.

Nigel is my life, my soulmate. I sat at his bedside in the hospital every day, 8 a.m. to 7 p.m., for fifty-six days and from 2 to 6 p.m. for his twenty-four days in rehab. I would have done anything to have him out of the hospital and back home.

We don't decide to become a loved one's caregiver; it just happens. We have no choice. I thought this would be something my husband and I would do for each other in elderly years. I admit, I got tired of the daily driving—thirty minutes to the hospital and over an hour's drive to rehab.

On December 23, Nigel was released from Sunnyview Rehab. I was overjoyed. I was willing, without hesitation, to do what was needed for him to get well.

The den in our home was on the main floor, so this was converted into Nigel's recovery room with a hospital bed and oxygen generator. I was given a list of all Nigel's medications, including dosage and time of day to administer them. I was given boxes of bandages, tubing, and ointments. The first twenty-four hours as his caregiver, I was overwhelmed. But, once a routine and schedule were in place, we began to get through this.

I learned how to clean the trach, flush and clean the feeding tube, and treat the bed sore at the base of his spine, making sure it healed from the inside out. I assisted Nigel with getting to and from the bathroom, with brushing his teeth, and with bathing.

In three weeks, Nigel's trach and feeding tubes were removed, and slowly, very slowly, he began to get back to living. Our lives were changed. Physically, he was no longer the man I married, but he was alive, and I was grateful.

2010 was Nigel's year to heal. He was back to work part-time in March, 2010, and by May, he was back full-time, although with limited stamina. I suffered a bit with post–traumatic stress, worrying every time Nigel coughed, concerned about him being around crowds, afraid he would catch a cold. Because of the damage his lungs took from the illness, even a common cold could put him back in the hospital.

In 2011, we began his travel engagements again. This time, I would travel everywhere with him, since he needed a bit more assistance. Instead of standing at a podium to speak, he needed to sit on a stool. He was out of breath a lot as his lungs tried to heal.

In September of 2012, Nigel had to have his right hip replaced. The steroids that saved his life in 2009 had caused avascular necrosis (death of bone tissue due to lack of blood), which is not unusual for someone who was given lots of steroids.

I was back to being a full-time caregiver again. I was exhausted. I found myself struggling. "Nigel must try to do more on his own!" I thought. "What about me?" I know there is nothing wrong with feeling this way. It's a part of "compassion fatigue," the emotional distress or apathy resulting from the constant demands of caring—a caregiver's burnout. Compassion fatigue has been defined as "a combination of physical, emotional, and spiritual depletion associated with caring for patients in significant emotional pain and physical distress."

I remember one of Nigel's occupational therapists in rehab telling me, "There will come a time when you have to step back and let Nigel do it himself, forcing him to become independent again." Nigel's becoming able to brush his own teeth or get himself dressed was a major accomplishment.

In March, when Nigel returned to work, he led a healing service for the first time since his illness. I was the one who introduced him. I kept my promise to the Lord that day, and I told my story, my testimony of God's healing of my husband. Since then, many people have asked me to speak on Nigel's illness, and I have been obedient. Now nearly six years later, I find myself having to share the experience once again. As distressing as it is, I will continue to testify for the Lord whenever He asks me. Introvert or not, I will keep my promise. I am eternally grateful.

"May the God of hope fill you with all joy and peace as you trust in him, so that you may overflow with hope by the power of the Holy Spirit."
(Rom. 15:13 NIV)

CHAPTER 10

What I Learned in the Hospital

I'VE SPENT TWENTY-FIVE years learning from people suffering from physical, emotional, mental, spiritual, generational, relational, financial, historical, locational, racial, inter-denominational, intellectual, national, international, and global issues of healing. I've had the privilege of visiting hundreds of people in the hospital.

In a hospital bed myself for three months, I learned the other side of things: the sudden shock of the lights turned on at 4:15 every morning for the daily draw of blood. When the veins are collapsed, the lady poking around with the needle for a vein can be most unpleasant. I would nap for a while until the daily routines began. Observing people from the bed, watching the visitors, became something I looked forward to.

A hospital visitor follows certain standard protocols, including making sure a visit is convenient for the patient, making sure the patient is available and not having medical needs attended to, washing the hands, etc. I was amazed at how people interacted with me. There were those who put their stuff on my bed and sat down, ready to camp out for the afternoon. There were also those with onion breath or copious amounts of perfume or aftershave, which made me sick. There was a person who stood at the eleven o'clock position of my bed. I knew a visitor was there, but because of the trach tube I couldn't turn my head to see the face; I was too weak to move.

Then there was the person who stayed way too long. Another sat in the chair and put his legs on the bed. There was the person who sat and said nothing, maintaining a holy presence, but for me the silence was deafening, as I was in physical pain. And there was the person who sat on my bed—a major no-no! Claustrophobic, I wanted to shout, "You are totally in my space, causing me pain; I cannot move under my own power, and the bed clothes are restricting me." With one word, one breath, I tried to direct the visitor to a chair.

I found myself trying to remember all the visitors' different quirks so I could assess the best way to visit someone in hospital. I really wish I'd had the strength to fill in a notebook. What a wonderful training ground for the future, as well as a way to get my mind off the fact that I had stuck a toothbrush up my nose, missing my mouth completely.

There was the person who kept touching and moving the bed. If I sat up, I felt extreme nausea; moving the bed made me seasick. There were those who were so shocked at my physical condition, they could not really deal with the visit at all and just stared. I felt like a medical experiment! "OK, so I've lost 58 pounds. I've been very ill; please don't stare."

And there was the person who came and did it right—kind, compassionate, with a quick prayer and away. I found myself wanting that person to stay longer. *(Thank you, Bishop David Bena.)*

All meant well, and I was grateful to so many who came. Still, I found it amazing to watch different personality types trying to learn to visit the sick. I tried to make it a way of passing the day, thinking I was one day closer to being able to reach my table, which the last person had moved so that my phone or ginger ale was just out of reach; one day closer to being able to sit up in bed; one day closer to being able to walk; one day closer to being sent home for Christmas.

Countless hours passed as I fixed my eyes on something, staring, brain switched off, awake, but in neutral. There were hours holding the hand of my dear wife, who brought me orange juice and stayed by my bed, 8 a.m. to 8 p.m. every day.

There were times when I prayed as much I was able, often leading me to nap. And there were times I was totally unable to pray. Those times were special, as I knew thousands of others were praying for me. I felt carried in prayer with a sense of warmth, knowing I was covered in prayer. I've met many who are in pain and who feel guilty because they're unable to pray. They often weep when I ask them if they're able to pray. There is a season for everything. When one is horizontal, the season is one of receiving.

There was a nurse, a lovely woman, who asked me about being a priest. She then asked me to pray for her, as her husband was doing life in prison. I remember the shock of hearing her words and then feeling tears run down my face, thinking about my own vulnerability. For the first time in weeks, I was able to pray for someone else. That was truly a heartfelt moment.

Then there were the perfect visitors, ones who would ask if this was a good time, ones who would assess the situation and come back later if I was being tended by nurses, doctors, or the ever-present X-ray machine.

The perfect visitor— I can see him now: quiet, compassionate, understanding, and able to sense the need and concern. I needed to try to make sense of this. I needed gentle spiritual direction and guidance. This visitor helped me process the visions I have written about in this book. He tuned in to what I needed and understood what I'd been through. When he visited, I felt that he had my soul in his hand. As I write about him now, I understand how to visit someone in the hospital. Many thanks to Bishop Dan Hertzog and Rev. Dr. Herbert Sanderson.

Dear soul, if you visit someone in the hospital, wash your hands before and after the visit.

Don't stay too long, and don't feel like you have to entertain the patient.

Ask if this is a good time. Sit or stand where they can see you.

Ask if you can do anything.

If you visit someone in the hospital, think about that person and their needs, not yours.

Passing a can of ginger ale from just out of reach is a very kind thing to do! (The ginger ale can always seems to be just out of reach!)

If you are comfortable, perhaps you might ask, "How may I pray for you?"

• • •

A Prayer for a House of Healing

"O God, make the door of this house wide enough to receive all who need human love and friendship and a Father's care, and narrow enough to shut out all envy, pride, and hate. Make its threshold smooth enough to be no stumbling block to children, nor to straying feet, but rugged enough to turn back the tempter's power. Make it a gateway to thine eternal Kingdom. Amen."

—Bishop Thomas Ken (1637-1711) (Written for some kind of healing place, or whatever passed for a hospital in those days.)

• • •

A Word on Convalescing

The very word *convalesce* seems to have fallen out of use. Why?

Convalesce: **verb, con·va·lesce:** *To become healthy and strong again slowly over time after illness, weakness, or injury.*

While I was convalescing, The Rev. Dr. Herbert Sanderson reminded me of the words of Isaiah: "This is what the Sovereign Lord, the Holy One of Israel, says: 'In repentance and rest is your salvation, in quietness and trust is your strength.'" (Is. 30:15 NIV) This was a foundational verse that I hung my healing upon.

Insurance companies kick people out of the hospital; we are expected to get back to work as soon as possible, perhaps because when we go in for surgery, we are back home before the end of the day.

If you can, take time to convalesce. Take a "time out" to recover. Be gentle with yourself, and please don't beat yourself up. So many people I meet beat themselves up. Give it up. The world does a good job beating us up; you don't need to join in. Let it go.

On Patient Advocacy

If you or a hospitalized loved one is not being looked after or you feel that you need to complain about something, ask to see a patient advocate—a trained professional who serves as a go-between for patients and hospital staff.

I was in the hospital during the rehab stage and had an awful pain in my right side. I was taken on a gurney to the ER for X-rays. After X-rays, I was parked in the corridor a long time, waiting from someone to take me back to the ward. I was plugged into the wall with oxygen into the trach, had no breakfast, and was lying on a very thin mattress. After waiting for hours, I was in a lot of pain in the area of the acute pressure wound at the base of my spine. I seemed to have been forgotten. I tried to get the attention of people passing by, but everyone had a destination. I had no cell phone. If I could have climbed off the gurney and pushed myself back, I would have. The pain was now very bad indeed, flesh complaining beyond words. I prayed my favorite prayer, "Help."

Then I remembered the words "patient advocate." I started calling out to everyone who walked by, as loudly as I could, "Patient advocate! Patient advocate!"

Meanwhile, Lynn had arrived and found I wasn't in my room. The nurses told her I'd been sent for X-rays —eight hours earlier! She went looking for me in the ER. Actually, she heard me calling for help before she saw me.

Finally, a patient advocate arrived, brought us lunch, and found somebody to wheel me back to my room in the main hospital. It turned out that I had been forgotten! That day I learned to be proactive. I did not complain; you understand; I just needed someone to hear me. Pain became the driving force for me to say those words as loudly as I could.

Someone once said that our adversities are God's universities. I learned a lot at the hospital university!

CHAPTER 11

Bible Connections

"But the wisdom that comes from heaven is first of all pure; then peace-loving, considerate, submissive, full of mercy and good fruit, impartial and sincere."
(James 3:17 NIV)

I HAVE NEVER once thought, why me? I have never questioned the Lord about why I went through such an ordeal. I've never questioned the call upon my life or asked why the Lord would take a former Drill Instructor, a Royal Marine, and put him in the midst of the healing ministry. This seems to be the path the Lord wants me to be on.

I can only think I went through the valley of the shadow of death, first with shell shock and then with swine flu, to come to know human suffering. For twenty–five years, while hearing thousands of people tell of suffering, I prayed for the wisdom and grace to understand. One can only draw upon one's own experiences in life. How else can one grasp such a mystery?

Bishop Dan Hertzog and Rev Dr. Herbert Sanderson helped me realize that each vision seemed to hang on a Bible passage. The H1N1 (swine flu) journey pulled me into the Word of God. For three weeks, my body could do nothing; it was as if it were dead. But my mind and my soul kept going, walking and living the Bible.

Psalm 23 (A Psalm of David)

The Lord is my shepherd; I shall not want.
He maketh me to lie down in green pastures: he
leadeth me beside the still waters.
He restoreth my soul: he leadeth me in the paths
of righteousness for his name's sake.
Yea, though I walk through the valley of the
shadow of death, I will fear no evil: for thou art
with me; thy rod and thy staff they comfort me.
Thou preparest a table before me in the presence
of mine enemies: thou anointest my head with oil;
my cup runneth over.
Surely goodness and mercy shall follow me all the
days of my life: and I will dwell in the house of the
Lord forever. (Ps.23, KJV)

• • •

My close encounter with death weaves together so poetically with Psalm 23. The Lord did make me lie down— not in a green pasture, but in a hospital bed where I saw green pastures. He did restore my soul and my body. The experience certainly changed my life, leading me down the right path with the Lord.

I had been down in the valley of the shadow of death before, but in the third vision I crawled down that valley. There was no turning back; there was no way up the valley sides. I was led by the Lord Himself, on the cross, encouraging me onward. When shown the dark pillars of hell on my left, did I fear that I was going in that direction? To be honest, yes. But He was with me, on the cross, guiding me. I crawled for what seemed like hours. Finally, with extraordinary effort, I glimpsed the pillars of heaven.

Reflecting on this, I wonder. If I had passed between the pillars, would I have stood up, completely healed, as I entered heaven?

When I try to make sense of this Biblically, not as a theologian but as 'heart–logian,' I realize that I was shown the very black pillars of hell for just a moment. I was given a second to pause, to ponder, to know that, just as "Heaven is for real," so is hell!

In the fourth vision, I sat at a long dark walnut dining table. There was nothing on it. The room was empty. I saw no enemies. I was at peace, waiting for the Lord to come in. The table was not yet prepared. It is only now, as I write this, that I realize the table was not "prepared before me." It was not my time.

I've been told that my head was anointed by many bishops and priests who visited me, and that three bishops gave me last rites. My head was liberally anointed with oil.

I have the assurance of goodness and mercy following me for the rest of my life. It is wonderful. This promise reminds us of the very gift of life, for us and for all people.

In vision five, I had a "fly-by" view of the many rooms of heaven. Now that I've seen, I have no doubt I will dwell in them forever.

What a gift it has been to experience such visions!

Having seen heaven, I ask myself, "Now what?" Tell the story, tell His story, the History. Let others know the beauty of what is to come, if we put right our lives, where we have strayed like lost sheep.

Perhaps we glimpse the pillars of Hades when we remember our sins. We stop, reflect, seek forgiveness, and we press on, not as victims, but as forgiven people. When we remember the Lord's incredible gifts and turn to Him, we are actually moving from victim to victor to victory.

May we pause here, dear reader, and take a moment to consider what I have just written. If you have been wallowing in the soup of victimization, if victim seems to be your identity, please get some help. Know that the Lord has not stamped Victim on your forehead. Go wash that off! Spend time with a new stamp: Victor. After a while, that will move to Victory.

Please don't permit others to have power over you. Rather, allow the Lord to gently empower you. He will pull you out of the valley of the shadow of death, heal the very core of your being, and put you in a place of life abundant.

"For if, by the trespass of the one man, death reigned through that one man, how much more will those who receive God's abundant *provision of grace and of the gift of righteousness reign in* life *through the one man, Jesus Christ!"* (Rom. 5:17 NIV)

I would also add, "Therefore, there is now no

condemnation for those who are in Christ Jesus." (Rom. 8:1 NIV)—a verse I find myself imparting to many souls who seem to be tortured by self-condemnation, self-blame and low self-esteem.

I've drawn so much closer to the Word of God through being close to death. It's incredible to realize that the visions relate to Bible passages. To think that I was being shown so much while in a chemically-induced coma! God really got my attention in the season of sickness and infirmity, allowing me glimpses of the world to come, made real in brilliant colors, so that the beauty of the heavens would become a vibrant, lasting memory.

"He will wipe every tear from their eyes. There will be no more death or mourning or crying or pain, for the old order of things has passed away." (Rev. 21:4 NIV)

Now I have no fear of death at all. When I go through this again, it will be very familiar. I have no doubt where I am going. I've seen it.

Perhaps you might ask yourself the question, "Do I know where I am going when it is my time?" Perhaps you might have a word of prayer asking God into your life, perhaps a prayer asking Jesus to be your Lord and Savior.

It has taken me six years to try and get my soul around all of this. Now when I see a beautiful night sky with bright stars, I smile. I've been up there. It's all beautiful. It is well with my soul.

Jesus said, "Peace I leave with you; my peace I give you. I do not give to you as the world gives. Do not let your hearts be troubled and do not be afraid." (John 14:27 NIV)

It all makes sense, Biblically.

CHAPTER 12

Recollections and Reflections

"Where, O death, is your victory? Where, O death, is your sting?"

"But thanks be to God! He gives us the victory
through our Lord Jesus Christ."
(1 Cor. 15:55,57 NIV)

WHEN I WAS a child, a three-foot model of *HMS Victory*, the ship commanded by Admiral Lord Nelson, was a treasure in our home. My father made that ship from scratch. I was a baby when my mother accidently dropped a hair dryer through the glass case and broke all the rigging. It took my father years to come to a place to be able to build the masts and rigging again. The model is now complete, and my father, "the Admiral," has made over 250 other scratch-built model ships.

There are times in our lives when we are broken, and there are times or seasons in our lives when we rebuild. May I encourage you to steer away from negative thinking and negative ways, to move from victim to victor. Enjoy the journey on *HMS Victory*. May I be a Barnabas, the son of encouragement, to move you from Victim to Victor to Victory.

The rabbi at a bar mitzvah I once attended told his students, "When you get to heaven, you will be asked three questions." I can't remember the first two, but the third question hit me right between the eyes. It was, "Did you have fun in your life?" My mentor and friend Francis MacNutt also told me, "Have fun." This is not a dress rehearsal! Get on with your God-given abundant life. And have fun on the journey. I thank God that He has given me a sense of humor. Sometimes you just have to laugh. "My God, my God, why have You forsaken me . . . Oh! There You are! You were there all along, in the wilderness of the Land of Coma."

While I was comatose, thousands prayed. My life was totally in the hands of God. As I crawled through the valley of the shadow of death, a nasty battle for my soul was underway. The prayers of the people conquered the foe; I have no doubt about that.

Before the H1N1, I had prayed, "Lord, I do believe; help me overcome my unbelief." (Mark 9:24 NIV) Now the Lord has led me through the valley of the shadow of death and healed, cured, and resurrected me. I know my Redeemer lives; I know who the healer is. I know the King of Kings, I know the Lord of Lords, I know the great physician; I know the lover of souls. Of this I have no doubt whatsoever. I confidently say, "Lord, I believe." Because I do.

Today, I travel a lot, leading healing missions around the globe. I make it a point to ask how many prayed for me when I was sick and to thank them.

On one of these occasions, I was literally cornered by three male medical doctors. I was standing, talking to someone, when three men came at me, faces very intent. I remember backing up as they approached, asking myself, 'What the heck is going on?' One seemed to be the designated orator, the other two encouraging him. They were on a mission.

"Did you know how sick you were?" was the first question. Then came a barrage of questions. "How did you survive?" "I want to know how you overcame such a dreadful diagnosis." "How on earth are you alive?" "Have you any idea all that was wrong with you?" "With even one of the issues you had, you could have died." And, "Do you know how blessed you are?"

All three doctors were Roman Catholic. They had followed the daily "Beth Strickland Report," and, as they read, they had agreed that I had no chance of surviving the ordeal.

Now they had a message to deliver. "We know what you went through, and all three of us are amazed." Intent on their mission, they closed in on me. They wanted me to know that I had undoubtedly received a true miracle from God Almighty.

We came back to the first question, "Did you know how sick you were?"

"Oh, yes," I told them, "I am very aware of what I went through. I even went to heaven five times!" I told them that I was grateful for their prayers, and I got the message. Then, much to their surprise, I asked, "How may I pray for you?"

In the end, I anointed their hands so they could pray for their own patients.

I've spent five years mulling over the visions, trying to get the fullest picture of the experience combined with the Bible's wisdom. I've found myself wishing that Lazarus, Dorcas, and all the Biblical people Jesus healed had written books on the subject. I'd like to hear more from those people who experienced what I experienced.

There are plenty of Bible passages about the healings—circumstances when Jesus prayed and healed the sick, but really not much about what happened after. The healing of the ten lepers in Luke tells us all were healed, but only one was cured, as he came back to say thank you. (Luke 17:11-19 NIV)

> "And whatever you do, whether in word or deed, do it all in the name of the Lord Jesus, giving thanks to God the Father through Him." (Col. 3:17 NIV)

To be so close to death and be brought back from heaven is not without major stress and depression, moments of euphoria, and moments of deep sadness. One looks at life through a different lens, trying to understand.

What really happened to Lazarus? What did he do? What did he talk about after his deliverance from death? Was he different towards others? I so want to know about his personal experience of being called, by name, out of the cave. He had been dead for four days, yet he heard the words of Jesus, "Lazarus, come out." He got up from his death bed and, still covered in the bandages, staggered out of the cave, much to the surprise of his sisters, Martha and Mary, and those gathered around him. At this point, Jesus told some people to help Lazarus out of his grave clothes. "He stinketh" was the word of the day.

I remember the feeling of my grave clothes falling off me the first time I preached, from a chair, nearly a year after my recovery. The spirit of death was leaving me, allowing me to return to life, and indeed life abundant, having witnessed heaven in all its glory.

I don't have recurring nightmares, but I do know that I have PTSD from the experience. It's a normal reaction to an abnormal situation. I do know that this life-and-death encounter has brought me much closer to God and to my amazing bride. I confess that depression has been a battle. My doctor, "Bones," told me, "Father, there would be something wrong with you if you didn't have depression after what you went through!"

I have a few daily reminders of my illness: the tracheotomy scars I encounter when I shave; three impressive scars on my chest; the tender flesh at the base of my spine. Residual pain in both my thighs serves to remind me of the suffering of our Lord. I walk with a cane, sometimes with a walker. I ride on an electric scooter in the mall and in airports or on the boardwalk. Because my lungs have been compromised with fibrosis, I am short of breath. Lung tests early in my recovery showed that I had only sixty-three percent of my breathing capacity—now improved, thanks be to God.

• • •

"We are hard pressed on every side, but not crushed; perplexed, but not in despair; persecuted, but not abandoned; struck down, but not destroyed. We always carry around in our body the death of Jesus, so that the life of Jesus may also be revealed in our body." (2 Cor. 4:7–10 NIV)

I've written about "Climbing the Cross," the vision I had shortly before contracting H1N1. The Lord asked me to lift Him up so He could breathe. He said, "I want you to see what I see,"—to look at everyone through His eyes to grasp the plight of the human condition, to fully understand the healing ministry.

Within weeks, I was hospitalized with respiratory failure. The Lord had died by suffocation. I was very close to death. The medical team had done all they could for me. A food cart was prepared for the dying man's wife and friends.

The tsunami of prayer began. I kept breathing.

Now I realize Christ was helping me to breathe. As I had lifted Him, so He now filled my lungs. It was as if He said, "You lifted my lungs so I could have one more breath, and I have breathed into your lungs the very breath of life." One collapsed lung was pierced, like the soldier's sword pierced Jesus, and a flow of fluid was released, restoring my ability to breathe. I am so humbled.

The Book of Acts is still being written; the Lord's healing ministry is alive.

I have a certain sadness closing this final chapter, but now I need to let it go and draw on my experiences to help others. Thank you for joining me in my journey through the valley of the shadow of death and into the peace and grace of healing. I pray that the words in this book have helped you to connect a few dots in the journey of your life. I pray that you have come a bit closer to the Lord of Lords. I pray that your fear of death might be changed into a supernatural peace. I pray for your healing in heart, mind, body, and soul.

I can now say, with holy boldness, the words of St. Paul:

"I know a man in Christ who fourteen years ago" (or in, my case, six years ago at the time of this writing) "was caught up to the third heaven. Whether it was in the body or out of the body, I do not know." (2 Cor. 12:2 NIV)

God knows . . . Of this I have no doubt.

Good Friday

Every morning I look at my face in the mirror to shave.

Every morning I see the tracheotomy scar on my face.

Every morning I think, "Wow, I am alive."

Every morning I thank God for answered prayer.

This morning, Good Friday, I look at HIS scars...

And thank Jesus that He died for me...FOR ME.

—Fr. Nigel Mumford March, 2016

ACKNOWLEDGMENTS

I owe an enormous gratitude to my ghostwriter extraordinaire, Lynn Dean Hunter, who brought me out of a six-month writers' block, for her expert guidance; to proofreader Beverly Foote; and to Cindy Shumaker Sholander, who also worked tirelessly on my third book, *After the Trauma, the Battle Begins, Post Trauma Healing.* All were invaluable in translating my British English into American English, while keeping my native language and train of thought intact. Without your help, dear ladies, this book would not be printed.

To John Koehler, my publisher, who was great to work with and one funny man. John, you made the process of producing this book fun.

My deepest gratitude to Sandra Lester, who stood by Lynn and me during all the infirmity, (thank you, dear Soul!); and Beth Strickland, who was tireless in keeping the global prayer team updated daily with information in how to pray for me.

Thank you to my doctors: Dr. Austin Tsai, MD, who stood by Lynn in extreme kindness through the weeks of despair; the pulmonary team: Dr. Carlos A. Ares, MD, Dr. Rodney Ying, MD, Dr. Desmond R. DelGiacco, MD; my amazing ICU nurses, Tasha Flint and Karen Lucas, who went totally beyond the mile to save my life; Mary Michalak, another of my amazing nurses; the many other nurses and staff of Saratoga Hospital who helped us through the battle and whose kindness touched my soul; and the OT and PT team at Sunnyview Rehab Hospital, especially Julie Buchan, for teaching me to brush my teeth and walk again.

Many thanks to the Rev. Dr. Herbert Sanderson, the Rt. Rev. Dave Bena, and the Rt. Rev. Dan Hertzog, who visited me, gave me last rites, and helped me process what happened from a biblical perspective.

To the faithful clergy of the Albany diocese, especially Fr. John Hopkins, Fr. Derick Roy, Fr. Joe Caron, and Fr. Chip Strickland (Beth's husband).

To the many dear friends of the Albany diocese who got on their knees, praying for my very life, especially Noel and Meryl Dawes; the Rev. Lynn Curtis; the Sisters of St. Mary's, and the many prayer warriors who came to the hospital lobby for the prayer vigil on Oct 23rd, 2009, the night the doctors said there was nothing more they could do.

Thank you to thousands of known and unknown people who prayed for me all over the world. I now understand the power and grace of "corporate prayer." To be the recipient of such prayer has been very humbling. I cannot possibly name you all. Thank you for saving my life.

ABOUT THE AUTHOR

The Reverend Nigel Mumford was born and educated in England. He is a combat veteran and former drill instructor with Her Majesty's Royal Marine Commandos. He came to the USA in 1980.

His call to the healing ministry came in 1990, after his sister, Julie Sheldon, was cured of dystonia through the prayers of the late Canon Jim Glennon.

Ordained an Episcopal Priest in 2005, Rev. Mumford founded By His Wounds, Inc., a nonprofit which hosts the Welcome Home Initiative, a healing ministry for combat veterans. The ministry has been presented at the Pentagon, as well as featured in *The New York Times* and on Christian Broadcasting Network.

In 2009, Rev. Mumford was hospitalized with Swine Flu (the H1N1 virus) and came "as close to death as possible without dying," as one seasoned doctor put it.

Fr. Nigel lives with his wife Lynn in Virginia Beach, Virginia.

OTHER BOOKS BY NIGEL MUMFORD:

Hand to Hand: From Combat to Healing. Church Publishing, NY, 2001.

The Forgotten Touch, More Stories of Healing. Seabury Press, NY. 2004.

After the Trauma, the Battle Begins: Post-Trauma Healing. Oratory Press, VA, 2011.

CPSIA information can be obtained
at www.ICGtesting.com
Printed in the USA
FSOW02n0707030417
32646FS